Me, My Pillow and Kicking Feet

by **Robert Creighton**
Illustrated by **Lindsey Martin**

ISBN 13: 978-0986031205
Text and Images Copyright 2012 by Robert Creighton.
All rights reserved.

Dedicated to

Bobby

and

Sean

Two of the world's most notorious pillow kickers

Father always told me
Father always said,

"Pillows are for your head,
and should remain on the bed."

I reached for the floor,
but it kicked out the door.

Across the grass and into the street
My pillow and feet continued to meet.

Down the road and around the block
My pillow and me out for a walk.

On to school before the bell
With my pillow in class all is well.

Off to the zoo my pillow and me
Apes, bears, and lions to see.

To the store with my pillow once more
Sliding along the shiny white floor.

Over my friend's to run and have fun
My pillow gets kicked by everyone.

Heading back home
we walk down the street
Me, my pillow and kicking feet.

Into the house and past father's chair...

Father comes walking with a long stride
He sees my pillow and it I can't hide.

My pillow was once very clean and quite bright
But has become rather dirty, an ungodly sight.

Father looks stern
and once more does repeat,

"Pillows are for your head,
not for your feet."

I pick up my pillow all dirty and worn, and hand it to father awaiting his scorn.

"What have you done?
Where has this been?
All over town by the shape that
it's in."

"To sleep with this pillow would be to get sick.
I know this pillow's been given a kick."

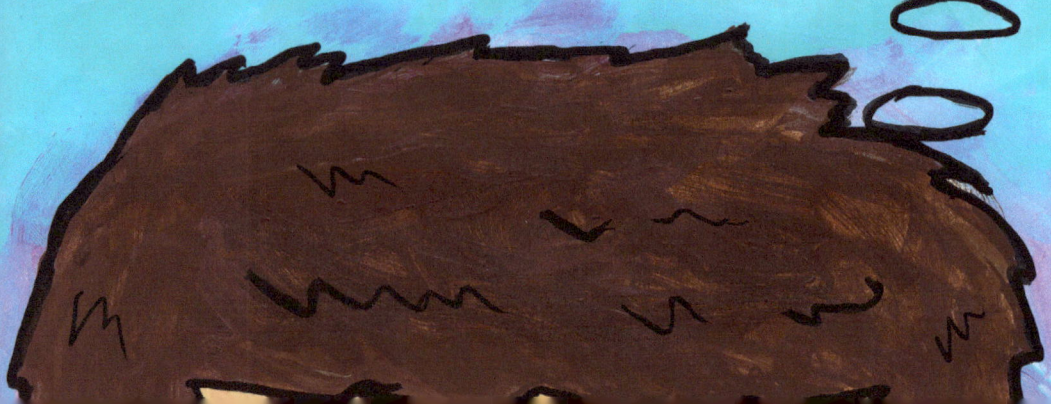

"Now this you must wash,
and this you must clean.
A pillow like this must never be seen."

He looks at my pillow and pulls off its case
He looks at me with a smile on his face.

With joy he kicks it to the floor

He kicks it again and kicks it once more.

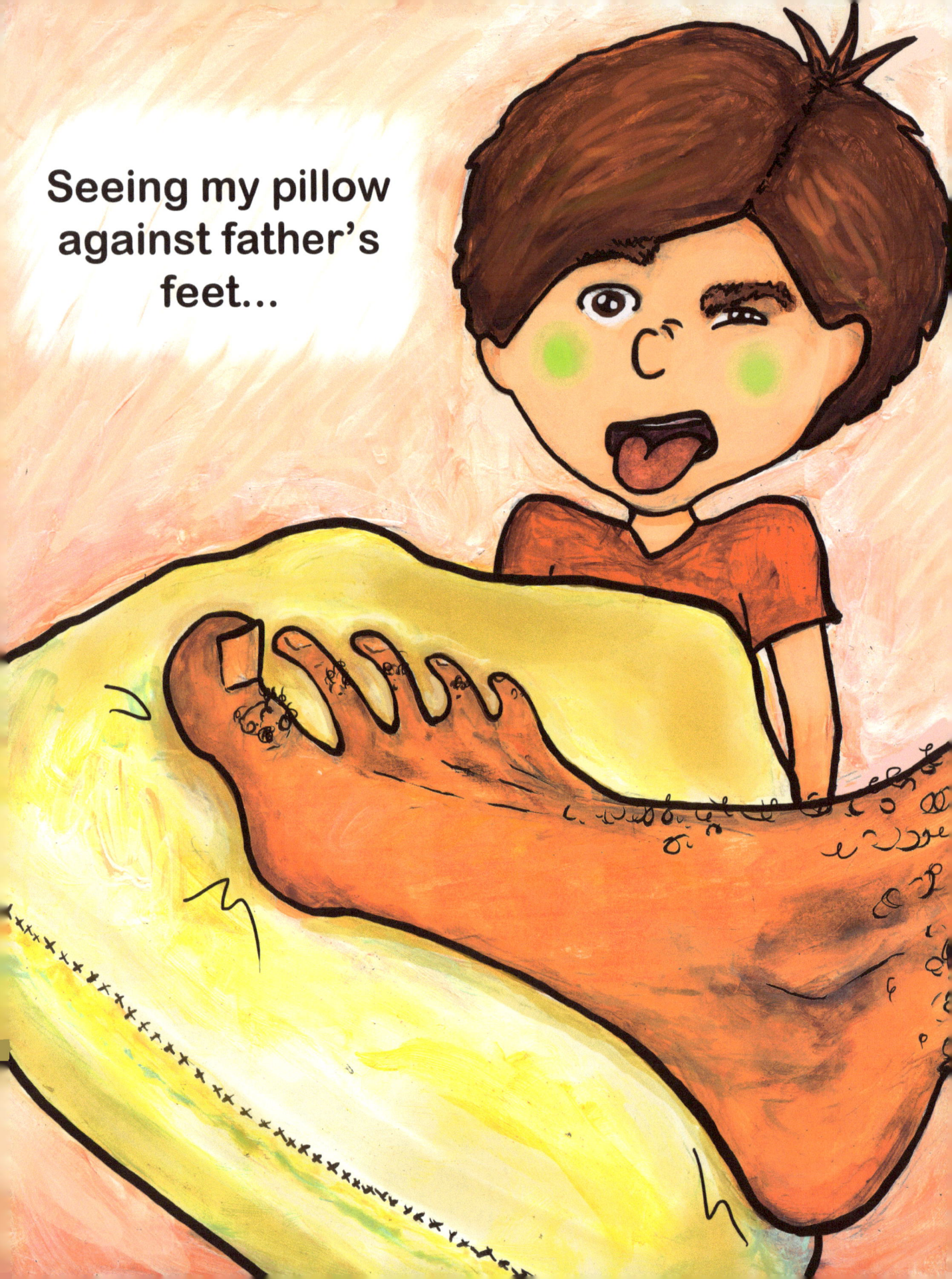

... I finally realize the two should not meet.

I then heard myself say
It was then that I said,

"This pillow's for my head,
it should stay on my bed."

About the Author

Robert Creighton is a Tampa area podiatrist and foot surgeon. He was inspired to write Me, My Pillow and Kicking Feet by his own children who often used pillows for play including kicking and stomping all over them.

As a foot specialist treating diseased feet all day it was especially difficult for him to see pillows on the floor that were later put back on the bed for potential use. This soon became a pet peeve that was the inspiration for this book.

Dr. Creighton is a 1988 graduate of The Pennsylvania College of Podiatric Medicine in Philadelphia, which is now the Temple University School of Podiatric Medicine. He received his undergraduate degree from the University of South Florida.

For more information go to CreightonWrites.com.

www.ingramcontent.com/pod-product-compliance
Lightning Source LLC
Chambersburg PA
CBHW041241040426
42445CB00004B/112